MW01170995

# God Is Greater Than Storms in Life!

## Up Lifting Poems

*Trust in the Lord with all your heart.*
***Proverbs 3.5***

***Written by: Verna D. Green***

# Table of Content

# Dedication

The desire in my heart that this book, Touch and will help every man, woman, boy and girl. Hopefully, the love of the creator will heal every broken heart. To all those that bless me with their time to read it, May the love of God let them trust and believe in it. The power of God's love can heal you and help you to want to change. Once the love of greatness is revealed you will never be the same. Just want to say thanks to those that encouraged me along the way. Betty Roston, Janell M. Green-Lassiter, Marene Austin, Mrs. Helen, Mrs. Katherine and Linda Longdon.

A special thanks to Mrs. Romona Golphin-Webb for connecting me with the right publisher. I couldn't have this without your help sister I believe this was a divine connection. Praise God, forever thankful. May the blessings of the Lord continually flow in your life. And a special thanks to Ms. Stacey.

# Acknowledgements

Writing this book was one of the most unbelievable things that I think I've ever done in my life. I know that it will help hurting people change their mindset about life. Life is what you make it to be. We have the power to choose.

First I want to give thanks to God for giving me another chance in life. I want to help make a difference in todays world. I thank God for being my educator, motivator and stimulator. Blessed am I for having wonderful parents in my life, forever I will love my late parents Milton Green Sr. and Lue Dessa Green. A Special thanks to my pastors Johnny and Gladys Hood.

Love always my family! My daughters and son Jacqueline, Kimberly, Jack, Stephanie, Mikessia and Kalandis. My grandchildren Jamien, JaNyia, JaMarkus, Jaylen, BryOnna, JaKylah, JaMarko, JaMya, JaNasia, JaMariay, Kyngston, Khaza, Royal, Legend and Rylan. My bonus children && grandchildren Kimberly, Sharika, Jack Jr., Shardae, Jariq, Kevryn, Kadee and Omari. Last but not least, a very special thanks to my Uncle Pap aka Sylvester!

# Introduction

How Great is our God, he is the greatest, the one and only Magnificent King of all living and dead?

As a firm believer, I have witnessed the power of God in many ways and on numerous occasions. He touched my great niece and healed her from a blood clot on her brain. When a clot showed up in her first X-ray, we prayed for her that God will be her Doctor and to operate on her without man lifting a finger. We prayed that he removes the clot from her in the form of a miracle happened.

With God all things are possible to those that believe with their hearts and with no doubt in their mind. To all those that seek, you will find. Let your spirit trouble not for if you wait a little longer, that you seek will be found. Hold on to your faith and touch others with kindness in what you say.

Love is greatest when it is received by those in need. To be frank with you, I believe that everyone needs and truly deserves to be loved. Trials and tribulations are a part of this life that we live. Therefore, spare yourself and strive to do only that in which you can do. Do your best and let God handle the rest.

# Learn how to encourage yourself

We have to learn how to encourage our self.

You cannot always depend on everybody else.

For me the Lord gave me Strength and the power to pray.

You must learn to put your confidence in the Lord.

This life can be easy or it can be hard.

And trust in the Lord will set you free,

from insanity and misery.

Help me Lord and lead the way.

I would love to see a brighter day.

Many times, doubt has come in and tried to steal my faith.

Remember you are always loved.

He created you as well as the earth and the skies of up above.

We must find out evil and stomp it out.

Live life to the fullest and smile along the way.

Love others the way you would want to be loved.

Take time out for kindness each day.

# After All the Things I Have Done

After all that I have done,

I am still loved by the Father and the Son.

You have tried to show me that I don't have to live bound.

Because of your love, my life has been turned around.

I feel freedom in praising my lord.

He keeps when life is good or hard.

You place so much love inside of me.

God you created me to be free.

Once I was blind and could not see,

Until your love opened me up to reality.

Always you have been present in my life,

Even through my triumphs, failures and strife.

After all that I have done,

You still love me.

My heart is filled with big dreams.


Sometimes life gets in the way,
I have learned to live by faith.
To make it in life from day to day,
Depend on the Lord and listen to what he says.
After all I have done,

You still guide me and keep me daily.

# Christ Will Open Up Doors

Life can be wonderful to explore.

Christ can give you one idea,

That will bless your life forever more.

He will open up to you a spiritual door.

His love will sit upon you like a dove.

A purity from up above will become yours.


The love of God is more precious than diamonds or pearls.

We are his and he watches over the whole world.

The doors he opens up cannot be closed.

Remember from the dead he was raised.

The Lord of host is with you every day.

# God gave us the breath of Life

Life is precious can you see.

It is what you make it to be.

Be happy and joyful all the days of your life.

Free yourself from struggle and strife.

Life should be wonderful for you and me.

Learn to let your mind be free.


God gave us the breath of life.

You can experience a peace that surpasses all understanding.

We all know that sometimes life can be demanding.

It doesn't matter what it is that you are going through.

Know that God is always there for you.

He will heal us from our hurts.

He will deliver us from our sins.

God is the captain of the team that wins.

# Why God Words Come?

God word comes to impact us.

The enemy comes to distract us.

God is trying to equip us.

Evil comes into our life to defeat us.

God word comes to purge us,

because he truly loves us.


God sends his words to cleanse us,

From the filthy flesh.

God spirit wants to come in,

To cleanse us from our sins.

It is up to us who we choose to let live within,

Our hearts, minds and souls.

He will heal us from our hurts.

He will deliver us from our sins.

God is the captain of the team that wins.

# Have You Looked for True Love?

Have you looked for love in so many places?

Looking for love in all the wrong places.

God love is starring you right in the face.

Have you ever looked for true love?

Did you think it was from the heavens above?


Have you tried hard to fill the emptiness in your soul?

It is hard to find true love in a world so cold.

God's true love opened my eyes, so that I can see.

I found true love inside of me.


Love is to care.

Love is to share.

Love is fair.

God's love teaches you how to prepare.

His love will always be there.

Have you looked for true love?

# REST PERFECT

R= Resist-resist the devil and he will flee.

E=Exalt-god will exalt you in dew season.

S=Shower-Christ will shower you with his blessings.

T=Temple-your body is the temple of god.


P=Power-there is power in praising our God.

E=Excellent-oh how excellent is though name.

R=Redeemer-Christ is the redeemer for the lost.

F=Faith-we should walk by faith not by sight.

E=Endure-Christ will strengthen you to endure trials.

C=Confess-confess your faults one to another.

T=Tithes-all tithes and offering belongs to god.

# Learning to Look Beyond

If you learn to see beyond your circumstance,

You will win your battles.

When you learn to trust God and live by faith,

You will realize that he always prepare a way.

Learning to look beyond what seems impossible,

Will help you see the possible.


Reflect on all that you have been through.

How did you get through all that life has thrown at you?

Who gave you the mind and strength to move forward?

Reflect on how your life came into order.

If you learn to see beyond your circumstance,

You will win your battles.

# P.E.A.C.E

P=Prayer-prayer helps you to become strong.

E=Everlasting-living for Christ, you will experience Everlasting life.

A=Angels-God gives you angels to encamp all around you and to protect you.

C=Compassion-have compassion for the needy.

E=Enter-to enter in you choose to be born again.

# Jesus Loves Us

Love will helps us to pray for one another.

In love we are sisters and brothers.

Love will raise us to another level.

Love will help to bring out the good and conquer the bad.

Why do Jesus Love us,

If we are not as good as we should be?


Love will help us to be on one accord.

Love will satisfy our Lord.

Love will teach us to be strong.

Love will lead us to live right and forsake wrong.

Father of all, sitting on the throne;

Has been looking after us all along.

Love is a powerful source.

Live your life in it and rejoice.

Love will produce fruit.

Love will let you forgive me and I will forgive you.

# Salvation Is Available to All

When we repent and turn away from our sins.

that is when salvation truly begins.

The spirit of love and truth will dwell within us,

teaching us to believe in a life free from sin.

To experience this joy,

One needs to be reborn again.

The Holy Spirit gives us strength,

That if we fall we can always repent.

God is faithful and he is just,

He would never give up on us.

Salvation is available to all,

One day your name will be called.

He delivers us from the wickedness of the flesh.

Put your trust in him for he lives in you.

To thine self be true.

Know your destiny is within his heart.

Stay Focus on God and His Word

Staying focused will teach you to be strong,

When everything around you is going wrong.

Staying focused will help you to grow.

It will reveal to you the things that you didn't know.

Staying focused will help you learn to love your enemies.

Staying focused will help you to succeed.

Staying focused will help you trust God to meet your needs.

Listen carefully to understand what you have heard.

Stay focus on God and his word.

Staying focus will teach you how to walk,

In the will of God with your whole heart.

Life will suddenly not seem to be so hard.

Staying focus will help you to always pray,

No matter what comes your way.

Remember there is only one way for true life.

God gave the world his best sacrifice.

# Give God a Life That He Can Bless

Will you give God your life, so that you can bless?

Ask the Holy Spirit to burn out ungodly mess.

This is the time to live and confess.

Let the love of God bring out your very best.

Wisdom is here to guide and comfort you.

The choice is yours to make, what will you do?

Give God A Life That He Can Bless.

All of us have a purpose.

I believe this to be true.

A long and prosperous life,

Can be obtained by the spirit of Jesus Christ.

We were brought out of darkness into his marvelous light.

Learn to live by faith and not by sight.

In this life we will have trails and tests.

Give God A Life That He Can Bless.

# God Created Special Women

Growing up in this world today.

I found it hard to know how to pray.

I really didn't know who I was,

Until God blessed me with his love.

A woman like me could not see,

Until he rest assured inside of me.

Now I am learning to be the woman that he created me to be.

Ordained and blessed, I now know how to love me.

God created special women.


I t doesn't matter what I may face.

My heart, body, mind and soul I will embrace.

Ordained and blessed, I now know how to love me.

God created special women and now I am free.

# Marvelous are thou name

Oh, it is wondrous at how his love remains the same.

Even as in life, there will be some sunshine and rain.

God's love will never change.

God is a marvelous name.


In spite of some heartache and pain,

There is comfort in knowing that his love is forever the same.

He walks with us in sickness, misery, love, happiness and every emotion.

A love that is pure and true devotion,

Belongs to God himself the creator of all things.

Forever and ever, he will reign.

God's love will never change.

God is a marvelous name.

# Nothing is impossible with God

With God we can truly live.

Through him our life will be fulfilled.

With him we can do all things.

He is the Lord of Lords and the Kings of Kings.

For in him we become complete.

Wonderfully created and individually unique.


God has given us the ability and the strength.

For us, his only begotten son he sent.

Let us as God's children be content.

All human beings will make mistakes, we must admit.

Fall to your knees and repent.

There is nothing impossible for God.

# God Can Do Supernatural Things

He created night and day.

God manifest himself in many ways.

The Lord gives you hope and that creates faith.

As his child you look forward to brighter days.

In this life, things can get complicated.

Tried and true, with patience you have waited.

Within this life, you see concrete evidence of the factual.

God is power and his life is supernatural.


Pick up the pages of your life and write a book.

Look up to God and say this too is good.

Let go of the past and build toward the future.

Don't let trouble consume you.

Remember, you have an army of love on your side.

Come into life.

Within this life, you see concrete evidence of the factual.

God is power and his life is supernatural.

# He is Alpha and Omega

He is the beginning and the end.

Christ has come to deliver us from within.

Great God, Jehovah Jirah.

Truly, he is a great provider.

Christ is all knowledge and power.

He is the beginning and the final hour.


Christ is the only way that we will experience victory.

He died for us sinners on Calvary.

You don't have to live in defeat.

Great God, Jehovah Jirah.

Truly, he is a great provider.

Christ is all knowledge and power.

He is the beginning and final hour.

# Christ is the Motivation of Life

It is a time to trust our Christ.

He is the one who sacrificed his life.

On a day preconceived, he shed his blood.

The Lord saved us with his love.

He brought us through tears and strife.

Christ is the motivation for life.


I never known a soul that he rejected.

He died for the wounded and sin infected.

Love prevailed on the day, he thought of you.

A savior that is merciful and true.

On Calvary, he shed his blood.

That is when he covered us with his mercy and love.

He brought us through tears and strife.

Christ is the motivation for life.

# Lord my Desire

Lord I desire to be more like you.

Help me to see this life through.

My heart is for you and I truly surrender.

Bring my mind back to you and help me to remember.

I know that your love is forever and true.

My mind, body and soul belong to you.

Rest assured and refined by fire.

Lord you are my soul's desire.


Lord I want you and I really need you.

Guide me both day and night.

Comfort me in the hard times in life.

My desire is to get closer to you.

You are my lamp and you are my truth.

Rest assured and refined by fire.

Lord you are my soul's desire.

# Blessed and not stressed

As a child of God, I will walk like I am blessed.

I have the power to overcome stress.

When surrounded by negative forces.

I reach for my love source.

Therefore, I become empowered with the word.

Stress flees from me as quick as a bird.

I am blessed and not stressed.

As a human, I will face life's test.


Marching on into my victory,

living life is where you will find me.

When surrounded by negative forces.

I reach for my love source.

Therefore, I become empowered with the word.

Stress flees from me as quick as a bird.

I am blessed and not stressed.

As a human, I will face life's test.

Walk in the true Love church

# This Long Hard Road I've Traveled

Never thought that I would make it through,

but I did because of you.

Never thought these years would come to pass,

but they did and I have grown at last.

Lord you know the many times that I have messed up.

Sincerely, your child thanking you for your love;

I have learned to bow my head and pray.

Daily I treasure my life each day.

Faith helped me to stay strong.

I thank you Lord for never leaving me alone.

Life lesson has helped me to learn,

that it is about love not how much you earn.

God loves all of his children.

With him in our lives we all are winners.

# God is Greater Than All Things

He is greater than any song we may sing.

The Lord is greater than summer or spring.

Oh' to know the joy that he truly brings,

is magnificent as he created all things.

He is greater than winter are fall,

remember that he created it all.

God is greater than you and me.

He is greater than what the eye can see.


God is greater than the house we live in.

He is definitely greater than all of our sins.

Lord you are greater than the flowers that grow.

You are greater than any type of weather,

because your love last forever.

How great you are, I cannot count your love and care.

I just know that you are always near.

# Loving Christ is a Sacrifice

Loving Christ doesn't mean a perfect life.

You will have ups and downs and struggle and strife.

With Christ you can learn how to live.

The Lord will teach you to let go and forgive.

A life that is full of love and praise.

Christ will lead you to happier days.

With God's love, you will learn how to treat others.

You will respect your father and mother.


Christ first gave us his love.

On Calvary he shed his blood.

Give your heart and learn to receive.

Live a life full of richness and don't be deceived.

Help me Lord to trust and believe.

Be you and stay blessed.

Loving Christ is the best.

# When God Bless You and Haters Come

Your blessings will produce some haters.

Don't let it stress you, because it could be a test.

Give your time, love and you will be blessed.

Never settle for doubt.

That is not what your life is about.

What God has for me is for me.

It can be true love or just another day to see.


When praises goes up, blessings come down.

Bless the pastor for I have been found.

Let God speak through the preacher.

Walk in the presence of God and be a true teacher.

Lift up the ways of the Lord and you will be lifted.

He will lift you into a new spiritual dimension.

Your soul will be ascended.

# God Is

The Lord is with every breath we take.

He corrects us when we make a mistake.

God helps us as we go through.

Truly, he loves me and you.

He is life himself.

There for you in trials and tribulations.

He guides you into patience.


It doesn't matter how you feel.

When it is said and done, God is real.

The naked eye cannot see,

What is cloaked in mystery?

# Jesus Answers Prayers

Let it be known to pray.

Be careful and calculus in your ways.

Even when you feel a little down,

Know that God is all around.

Prayer can strengthen you.

Prayer can lead you to truth.


Prayer is a powerful tool.

Learn to use it and be careful in what you do.

Don't give up and please don't faint.

Grow from a sinner into a saint.

We are fearfully and wonderfully made.

He loves us from the moment we begin until the grave.

Christ came to meet all of our needs.

Take life with a song and be relieved.

# Jesus Blesses All Mankind

Jesus will come into your life and save you.

He will help you overcome as you go through.

The Lord really loves us.

Give him your heart and in him trust.

He paid the ultimate price.

Be grateful for your life.

Jesus blesses all of mankind,

Giving of his love and time.


The Lord has set us free.

Free to live righteously.

He is awesome and has all power.

Let him save you, minute by minute and hour by hour.

He paid the ultimate price.

Be grateful for your life.

Jesus blesses all mankind,

giving of his love and time.

# Learning to Trust God

It is in wisdom that we learn to trust God in the good and bad times.

No matter what we go through,

We have a helper in you.

I trust in you, my everlasting king.

You are heaven and earth, the reason that I sing.

It is confusing as times sometimes get hard,

but I have learned to trust God.


My life is blessed even after the heartache and pain.

You kept me from going insane.

I looked for love in all the wrong places.

I searched for love in so many faces.

You kept me from losing my ground.

I thank you Lord for being around.

It is confusing as times sometimes get hard,

but I have learned to trust God.

# Lord My Prayer Today

Lord my prayer today,

is for mercy and to find my way.

God let my life be a burning light.

Keep me in the fight.

I pray that we come to grasp,

and free each other from the past.


Lord my prayer today,

is to be stable and true.

I hope to see my life through.

Guide me Lord in all that I do.

Let me live by faith.

I will live in the moment of each day.

# No longer Blind

I used to be blind and now I see.

That God brings out the light in me

I once was in bondage and now I am free.

Free to live my life wisely.

I used to be lost and now I am found.

One day I will wear my everlasting crown.

Now that I place value on my time,

I live life and I am no longer blind.


I use to not no love and now I have love,

freely the Lord gives from up above.

I once was lost deep in sin.

I am now free from within.

God has moved miraculously in my life.

I can challenge my struggle and strife.

Now that I place value on my time,

I am no longer blind

# The Fountain

There is a great and life flowing fountain.

Sitting on a golden seat is a great king.

I heard that forever is his reign.

The best thing to ever happen to us is him.

Drink from his fountain and live.


Looking into his kingdom is magical and exciting.

We all are invited.

There is an invitation for you and me.

The one sitting on the fountain will set us free.


The fountain is made up of stainless steel.

Everything is alive in this kingdom, because it is real.

There is a great and life flowing fountain.

Sitting on a golden seat is a great king.

I heard that forever is his reign.

The best thing to ever happen to us is him.

Drink from his fountain and live.

# Not Enough Time

Time seems to be never ending.

I need to step back and see life for what it is.

Through all of the adversity, I have learned to see life as a gift.

For ever praise in life there is a shift.

It can shift the way of our minds.

Even as we feel there is not enough time.


We don't have enough time to relax and be free.

Not even enough time to feel all of God's security.

Need some time to think and regain my energy.

I know God has enough time to take care of me.


Will life be worthy without truth and spirituality?

Look around you and you can see it in reality.

Learn to seek life wisely,

because God's love is the only thing that can justify our souls.

# Standstill

Stars do twinkle and glow at night.

A gentle breeze can snuggle a soul just right.

The still of the sky can calm the mind and block out distractions.

Relaxation of the body, mind, and soul is pure satisfaction.

A standstill has embraced your soul.

The love God has for you is never on hold.

Be quiet and just stand very still.

Listen to that soft voice whisper from the air, I love you my child.


We are all individual with obstacles in our way.

God created us all equal and unique.

Remember, glory has been placed in your reach.

Therefore, humble yourself and be meek.

Some of us are strong and some of us are weak.

Standstill and help your sister and brother.

Standstill and take heed to the advice from your father or mother

# Reaching for a Star

Though, I am small to the naked eye,

my faith is not measured by my size.

My spirit will soar high.

Even in adversity, I will rise.

It doesn't matter who you are.

You have the right to reach for a star.


Reaching for a bright and shining star,

it will draw closer to you at God's altar.

Look inside you for your insight.

Stand on your own two feet and live life.

Reach for your star and define your purpose.

Kneel and ask for the right to see the true you.

You are unique and beautiful from the start.

Grab your star.

# In spite of what I see

Life can be long or life can be short.

Life can be easy or life can be hard.

Everyone has some types of issue.

Tearjerkers in my eye please pass me a tissue.

God will always be there for you or me.

He loves us, in spite of what we see.


God is bigger than life itself.

So put your worries up on the shelf.

Live your life to the fullest.

Learn to love you and treat yourself with grace.

In spite of what we see, God will never turn a way.


Within this life we must learn to grow.

Be kind to others for you reap what you sow.

Let your spirit soar across the sky and be free.

For you are loved, in spite of what you see.

# God of the Universe

He is everlasting and he is infinity.

Everywhere you look, you can surely see his hand in everything.

God is God all by himself.

His mercies, grace, love and kindness is seen throughout all creation.

Learn to trust and put that which should be first, first.

Know that he is the God of the universe.

He created the heavens and the earth.

God is universal; you can see him everywhere you go.

He is you and me, so put what should be first, first.

His hands extend to all and his love is boundless.

Let the mystery of love come into your heart and settle you.

It is up to you to learn your own truth.

# Rejection will come

At some point you might get rejected.

How will you handle it and how might you be affected?

What will you do, if someone hurts you?

Would you run and hide?

Can it affect your pride?

Especially when you haven't done anything to them,

and you count of them as one of your friends.

Rejection will come to all not some.


Be careful not to push others away.

Don't get caught up in what people have to say.

Don't allow others to steal your joy.

Love them anyway, because you have the power to.

Keep the focus on what you do.

You must not let others cause you to react,

even when you are unfairly attacked.


Rejection will come, for all not some.

Hold your head up high in the midst of chaos.

Do not let rejection stop you from being you.

Search for your own internal truth.

# Don't give evil an opportunity

You have power inside of you.

Learn to use it wisely and be careful what you do.

Never give your enemy an opportunity to hurt you.

Refuse evil and all the destruction that it could cause.

Give it to a higher power that rules all.


To reach your dreams, you have to learn to dream.

You must take action and bring your dreams to reality.

Don't give evil an opportunity to steal your joy.

It's up to you; you have the power of choice.

Within life you must learn to take the risk.

The risk of going after your dreams and living,


You were born with a purpose.

Learn who you truly are.

Many of you are a shining and bright star.

Don't give evil the opportunity to stop your destiny.

As a human being, you must learn to be free.

# The rain

When the rain pours it comes down, sometimes fast and sometimes dripping slowly.

It does not fall down to drown but to nourish all living things.

The rain is refreshing to those that it touches.

To sustain life, it means so much.

God ordains the rain to cleanse and wash away sins.

With the love of God, you will always win.


Let it rain, let it pour, the power of God keeps me coming back for more.

As I walked in life with my head held high.

I come to realize what life is and it's all about love.

Purify yourself with love and accept yourself for who you are.

Make your own movie and be your own movie star.

The sacrificial lamb has given all for all.

Therefore you can get up after you fall.

The rain will come and the rain will go.

A seed will grow to nourish your soul.

Remember, even in the midst of your pain.

Let go and let it rain and let it rain.

# The cooling waters of the soul

In this life we face struggles and strife.

We need something that heals the soul.

Life is a battlefield and in battle you learn to grow.

Sometimes we hurt, sometimes with cry and sometimes we laugh.

Never knowing the reasons why.

Throughout all, sometimes we are hot and other times we may be cold.

Let the rain fall, I want to feel the cooling waters of the soul.


The breath of air is a wonderful gift.

It is not something you can earn, it is what it is.

Love is not one-dimensional,

But God's love is intentional.

He is the cooling waters to every soul.

The love he gives would never get old.


God is God, and God is good.

He is Almighty in love and true to everyone.

He is the giver to humanity, his only begotten son.

Love lives on high and settle conflicts down below.

He is the master, the cooling waters to your soul.

# Changing times

Catch me; I am fallen from on high,

crying tears of joy and pain with no reasons why.

I march to the beat of life.

Praying to walk freely into the sunlight.

Overcome all of my obstacles it take flight,

looking forward to a new day that is shining bright.

Fly away with me on Eagles wings,

Changing times with life comes many things.


Look at why, you blinked and now gone.

Don't worry love will return me home.

God you have broken my heart of stone.

With love comes changing times,

For ever free or entrapped by my mind.

Creator, create a new heart and renew my soul.

That the stony roads will teach in reach those in need.

Changing times is what I constantly see.

# Never

Life is a struggle and I am a fighter.

Many times I have wondered will I make it through.

God knows I lost my way over and over again.

I look for the good even though I sin.

Never will I grow if I don't make any mistakes.

Never will I learn if life was always great.

Listen to my heartbeat that means I am alive.

Don't try to impress me with jive.


Never will I know if love is good if I don't seek it.

Never will I reach a goal if I don't set standards to reach it.

Life is about choices and sometimes we make good ones and sometimes we make bad ones.

Through it all God has our back for we are his daughters and sons.

Never will I know that the Sun shines Bright if I never looked into the sky.

Never will I know life if I don't live life.

God is good and I know that but I am human and I know that to.

I'm supposed to make mistakes that's what humans do.

# Risen

Life rises up inside of me and I become the living.

Every breath that I take is giving back into the living cycle of life.

For I have risen from my sleep.

Now I am searching for that I see also shall I reap.

He has arisen and he is the reason that I am what I am.

Individual and unique, I am what I am created to be.

Everyone has to story to be told.

Fear we keep some down in others will be bold.


Rise, my Lord of the Lords and let me be the host.

For are the one that I seek the most.

I know why mistakes are made and that's good.

It's all about growth in living life to the fullest.

God is a forgiving God and he holds no grudges.

He is the centerpiece of my life and he gives me water for my soul.

Risen, from the ashes of the Earth to a new place beneath the sky,

God is the reason that we have life..

# Glory all Glory

I need you every day.

You are the sun and the moon.

Feeling the love you give touches me in every way.

Without you my life is dark and full of gloom.

To you will be the glory forever and always.

Glory all glory, to the creator that creates.

Glory all glory, to the one who forgives me for each mistake.


I want a life that I can say that I lived.

A life that gave back to me and one that I can feel.

Let me be that in which I am created to be.

Love is intangible yet within reach.

Glory all glory, to the one who is, was and always universal.

His love of mankind is the epic love story.

It is the greatest love story ever told.

To the one that give his only begotten son to a world so cold,

Glory all glory be to God.

# In his eyes

Within God's eyes I am wonderful crafted and beautifully made.

He looked up on me with favor and kisses my skin with his sun.

For my love is his and he is the only one,

to seal with love that is the greatest thing I ever have known.

No secrets, no lies in any mind games.

My heart is his to be tamed.


In his eyes, I am beauty, perfection and a work of art.

He gives to me that in which no man can tear apart.

Love has no boundaries with I am with him in my heart and soul is open.

Raindrops falling gently from the sky inches into my spirit and give me all the reasons why.

I know life has no limits and I am without limits.

I treasure every moment, every second, every hour and every minute.

Within Gods' eyes I am treasured and appreciative to be lifted.

The spirit of my ancestors as a constant reminder that there was life before me,

And life will go on after me because this timeless.

Therefore, the of for each day,

And I hope and I pray for longevity.

For ever I am in his eyes.

# To Whom

To whom it may concern,

I am a human put on earth to learn.

Gentle creature that I am,

I am formed from woman and man.

Love has no limits, when you love yourself;

It is a key to true love and truly loving someone else.


To whom it may be of interest to.

I am me and you are you.

Wonderfully and fearfully made,

molded from Clay.

Look in the mirror and embrace your mind, body and soul.

For it is yours to behold.

# Treasure

Every day that I live to see is a treasure.

There is nothing in life but love that truly brings pleasure.

I searched the whole world and I cannot find,

a love like God has for humankind.

Touched by Angel and descended from the flesh.

My life is full of ups and downs; sometimes it is a mess.


Treasure the days that you live to see,

For tomorrow is not promised to you or me.

Enjoy the time that you have on our earth.

In truth your time start taking at birth.

Receive all the good things that God has for you.

Live in the light and embrace your truth.

Treasure all of your fond memories.

Accept all that you can be.

Live your life as if it's the last day that you will live.

Take what is good for you and always remember to give.

Treasure all your days,

Live your life in a special way.

# Family

God gives us a treasure called family.

The life's ups and downs,

be thankful to have family around.

Family is a gift to comfort and to help us grow.

They are the seeds to our life and the water to our soul.

There is nothing like a family that prays together,

because in the end they will stay together.

Their love will outlast the stormy weather.


Family is such a beautiful sight to behold.

They are the music to our life and a mystery that unfolds.

Treasure the gift of love.

Love is from on high up above.

Give yourself over to love, peace and comfort.

Family will be with you at every moment.

# Greater Love

So many phony loves came in and out of my world.

Each one took a lot from me and left me feeling alone.

I am tired of living life all on my own.

What I need is a love that is true.

I need a love that I can fathom and we will bond together like glue.

The stars cannot match this feeling from up above,

It's so real that my heart has been touched by greater love.


The script of my character and the River of the water that cools my thirst;

For the creators love I do not have to rehearse.

Your love took me by storm.

The love you gave gathered me from the cold and brought me into the warmth.

There is no greater love than you.

Before you I had not a clue in life for what I was supposed to do.

Lord, you are the master key in my heart you have unlocked.

Now you are with me as we look into your world of a greater love.

# Free

I was Cage once by my many mistakes.

Life is no fairytale, when love turns into hate.

No longer could I just exist I needed to live.

Something within me was struggling to break free.

I have to learn to take as well as give.

Free, free me oh Lord.

The pain of oppression is hard.


Hold me close and guide me through life.

Engage my mind, body and soul.

Deliver me from the world grown so cold.

Touched my heart and mend it with love.

Let grace fall down upon me from up above.

Free, free me oh Lord

The pain of oppression is hard.

# Faith and Grace

Faith and grace works together,

It will be hard to live by one without the other.

Some people seems to have the wrong motive about grace,

They think it gives them the license to sin,

I will say to you; that information is not true.

When you have fallen in love with the one who created you.

# We Have the Power to Choose

The things that we choose to do in life,

If it's bad you will pay a price.

I will encourage you,

If someone comes up to you to speak a little wisdom,

And it is true,

Listen because wisdom is good for me and you.

Something bad must have happened in their life,

And they didn't listen so they paid a price.

Maybe they have to live with it,

For the rest of their life.

Wisdom is a powerful tool and when you choose to receive it,

Pray he will give you the power to never lose it.

# He Saved My Life

He saved my life; you may ask me how,

when he gave his only begotten son; Jesus Christ.

That's how he saved my life.

And if you ask me what he saved me from,

I will say to you; self-destruction, drowning in my own sins,

I was destroying myself within.

It's truly a blessing being born again.

His love has truly restored me,

My eyes have been open now I see.

What a great sacrifice, giving his own life.

For a wretch like me.

# Prayer Elevates You

I am learning how prayer and praise builds you,

When you find yourself going through a storm?

That you don't have the answer to,

Just know his grace and mercy is renewed each morning.

If we learn how to keep our minds stayed on thee

The bible says that he will keep us n perfect peace.

Sometimes it will be a challenge, you'll see,

There're so many distractions

In this world that life throws at you and me.

But we win!

Christ has already given us the victory.

# Keep the Faith

Faith helps you to press through

The heartache and pain,

Will help you to accept the things in life

That we can't change.

And his grace towards us will always remain.

We have to learn how to accept

The things that has happened in life,

That will cause us to experience the power of change.

But his love, mercy and grace

For us will never change.

# Be Careful

Don't be so quick to throw the first stone

Have you ever asked yourself?

Why do some people act like they're up so high?

Sitting on a throne waiting on you to mess up

So they can throw the first stone.

Remember the woman who was caught committing adultery

And the people acted so happily that they wanted to stone her.

Religion is so quick to stone us,

And will try to be the judge for us

When they need to take a look back

And see that none of us have arrived yet.

We are all a work in progress.

# Power in Your Tongue

Watch what you say when something in life doesn't seem to go our way,

Learn how to speak over yourself,

Instead of always depending on someone else.

No I'm not saying that we won't need help along the way,

I'm saying that we have to hold on to our faith.

No matter what in life may come our way

Speak what you want and you will have what you say.

Don't live by feelings because feelings do change,

Learn how to live by faith and your situation will change.

# Experiencing Setback

You may be experiencing in life a seasonal setback,

Where things seem to be looking down,

And you feel that there's no help around.

Learn how to lift your head up

And encourage yourself instead

Don't always depend on someone else

Press forward within yourself

Into your comeback from your setback

# Saved People Go Through

We all have some challenges in life

Just because were saved doesn't mean things will always
go right

The way we want it to

But just be thankful for how much he loves me and you

He has opened up our blind eyes to see

The price he paid for us to be free.

Way back on Calvary!

# Backsliders Come Back!

Remember what he did when he bleed

That's how much love he has already spread

No excuses for keep sliding back

Because his arms are open wide,

Saying I love you my child,

Come on back

# Change Is Needed

When you're going through

Have you ever stopped to think?

Why some things are happening to you

Do you think it could be that?

A change needs to take place within you

Change can be good for you and me

To help better yourself to be all you can be

There's help if we want it

Do you think if we could have changed ourselves?

We would have already done it

Nothing you tried to do could change me or you

Only the creator has the power to do.

# Be Thankful

Let's be thankful for the sunshine and rain

We will all experience these different seasons in life

To help us grow in our savor Jesus Christ

There will be winter, spring, summer and fall

On this earth you will experience them all

# Spotlight

Living a Christian life

The world chooses to have their own special spotlight

Watching to see, can a human being on earth live right

We are here to be a witness

Our righteousness is not of us

Be careful and don't allow yourself

To be quick to judge us

Because we are here to encourage you

That the creator truly loves you too.

# Don't Accept the Curses

There's generational curses that life try to attack us with

What I mean about that

Saying you will die with this or that

In life eyes, that's a fact

Salvation tells me that's not true

I shall live and not die

So I can testify

He has promised me long life here on earth

To enjoy life more and more

Joy flowing like a river

He is thee greater provider

There's no other beside him

# Weep Only for A Night

Weeping enduring for a night

But joy comes in the morning right

You might be going through a very hard situation

Could be causing you to lose all patience

Then begin to experience some sleepless nights

That your physical body lose the strength to fight

But keep the faith

Remember weeping only endure for a night

And joy comes in the morning right

We walk by faith and not by sight

# Being A Christian

Living a Christian life is for me

Even though I haven't dotted all the i's or crossed every

t

I know from experience he truly loves me

None of us will be perfect

But growing into perfection will be worth it

Wisdom says to repent

He has the power to forgive and forget

# Remember in Life

Remember that we all go through life

There's a purpose for me and you have a purpose too

Here on earth

Life doesn't promise me and life wont promise you

But when you decide to connect with the one who created you

Learn how to count it all joy

When temptation comes

That's the time to turn your back on

Because in the spiritual realm your battle has already been won

# Debt Free

It is a time to see

Yourself debt free

Believe it, receive it

If you can't see it

You will never be

Debt free

That is the same as having a habit

That seems so hard to break free

Just learn how to see yourself already delivered

And the battle has been won

He died for the whole wide world to be free

But the choice was left up to you and me

See yourself already debt free

# Accept Change

We have to learn how to adjust to life

Each season you could be experiencing

Some doubt and maybe a little bit of unbelief

And find yourself asking the question,

Why is this happening to me?

Can someone tell me please?

What is this reason, I'm going through this season?

The things that I've been through

He gave me the grace and power to write a book

That will encourage others like me and you.

# There Is Something to Learn

Through the storm there is something you should learn

It will teach you how to have patience

And open your eyes to see the revelation

Why you're experiencing the storm

You want to be a better you

There's grace in this race

In spite of the distractions we face

That has been set before me and you

In this life there will be some, that's true

Praise your way because you will get through

He will keep us safe and warm

Protecting us from all danger and harm

# Storm Doesn't Last

When you have a storm that you're going through

In life there's something that needs to change

If you want to succeed and gain

What he said is ours

Because he has given us all power

What power?

The power to get wealth and wish above all else

We be in good health

And know that there comes a point in life

You can be free

To live your life more abundantly

# Kneel and Pray

Have you ever felt like the whole world was tumbling down on you?

And the pressure was so heavy that you didn't know what to do?

Found yourself praying for his help to make it through

When it felt like all odds were stacked up against only you

There will come a time in your life

You will learn how to press your way through

Then look back on the storm and say thank you

For helping me come through

Because of his grace

I stayed in the race

# Lost Souls

You might be living in the middle of dark dark place

Allow Christ to use you to encourage others

This is the time to get saved

Some will say when I'm ready then I'll come

Just know none of us are promised to see another day

We are still here because of his grace

When your time is up what can you say

Breath leaves your body then its too late

Just because of the choice you didn't make

# There's A Beginning

When you made a choice to accept Christ

He is the beginning of true life

The middle is when you begin to experience change and grow

No matter what happens

His love embraces us the most

It is finished from the beginning until the end

He has already died for us to be born again

What an awesome friend we have

Since we made a choice to be free from bondage and sin

Because we made a choice to be born again

# Why Complain

Why do some of us complain?

Take a look back and see how he bore our sickness

And how he bore our pain

Have you ever asked yourself?

Why should we mumble and complain?

Think about how he took upon himself the whole world shame

Be sure to think about it before you decide to complain

# Patience Preserves You

Patience teaches you how to endure hardships

And will help you grown along the way

And show you that we need to always pray

Sometimes you may find yourself forgetting to pray

And he knows

Be thankful for his mercy and grace

Just know, when we are honest with ourselves

It will not be so hard to be honest with someone else

# Teach Me

Teach me to look beyond the faults of others

And show us how to truly love one another

We all have a destiny to fulfill in spite of the things we may see

The creator, he's the only judge for you and me

So will you choose to love me unconditionally

That's what God bay love means to me

That when I make a mistake, we all do,

Will you express your love towards, faithful and true?

# Life

Sometimes people think life is a game

Be careful, it just might cost you some heartache and pain

There comes a time to stop playing like life is a game

And grow up and stop costing yourself unnecessary pain

Time isn't waiting on you and time isn't waiting on me

Remember there comes a time in life, you have to face up to your responsibility

Life isn't a game!

# Live

You have to learn how to live one day at a time

Why worry about tomorrow?

You may find yourself full of life sorrow

I'm finding out that worry doesn't change anything

It will cost you somebody stress and a whole lot of pain

Cast your cares upon him

And learn how to live one day at a time

# Money Solves All Things

It is good to have money but don't let money have you

Don't put your trust in money because the love of money can destroy you

Some people uses it to buy a fleshy temporary love that isn't real or true

It is the devil! He's only playing you.

Because he isn't going to tell you the danger behind what he's doing against you

I'm exposing that this is what the love of money will do

If you fall in love with money

It can destroy you and other people too.

Remember solves all things

Don't fall in love with it

But he does want us to enjoy it

It can pay your bills and put you in a house to live.

# Ask

Have you ever asked the lord to make a way?

When there seems like there's no way

Well I found out the answer to this question is to trust and obey

When you choose to obey his ways

Keep the faith and believe the abundant promises will come your way

Because you made the decision to walk by faith.

# Give A Child

You might find yourself trying to give a child some wisdom

Even though he/she has become grown

So they won't in life keep going wrong

Sometimes wisdom might tell you to back off and leave them alone

We have to learn how in this situation to just keep prayer going on

# Why Worry

Worry is a defeat

That's used by the trick of the enemy

To keep us bound and block us from walking in true victory

It will cause you to repeat in your mind over and over again, the lies of the enemy

Worry blinds you from seeing the truth

What the word of the Lord says about me and you

His word will keep us in perfect peace

If we learn how to keep how mind stayed on thee

# Fear Can Change You

The fear of the Lord is the beginning of true life

His fear comes to lead and guide you

Into the right direction for your life

And the wisdom to avoid unnecessary strife

Don't be a person trying to find yourself judging everybody life

Pray for them that they will have a chance to get it right

Remember we walk in darkness before making the choice to come to the light

Now our eyes have been open to serve our savior right

Just pray that they won't let it be too late for them

to allow him to help them get it right

just keep encouraging them to come to the light

# Troubles

You might have some life troubles coming from every side

Where the enemy has attacked you from the blind side

Meaning something you didn't see

And you begin to ask yourself how did this situation sneak upon me

I know the word does live within me

I thought my guards were up so how could this be

Sometimes things will happen to help open our eyes to see

Pay attention, because the enemy has no love for you or me.

# Gifts

Your gift will make room for you

And will open up some doors too

But don't be so caught up in the gifts Christ has given you

Because the devil knows how to operate in the gifts too

Now remember he was an angel of light before that's true

Please don't allow the gifts to deceive you

Know that you are saved

And you're operating the gifts that God gave

# If You See

Now if you see me looking and feeling a little bit low

Don't try to judge me like you really, really know

I could need some help along the way

Sister or brother just pray

Lift me up towards heaven this day

And to encourage each other that something good is coming our way

# Storms

These are past storms I have been through

And the enemy spoke through my mind and said, "Ha ha ha this storm will be the death of you.

Then I begin to look back and realize

It was the devil lies that tried to deceive me

Because he knows that the Lord has great things in life for me

Learn how to speak good over yourself

Instead of believing the lies of what the enemy says

Remember there is power in the words you say

It might not show right then but I will encourage you to be aware

This is the wisdom in my heart to share

So be careful of what you speak

Because it will come into reality

# An Abusive Man

You may have a daughter that's experiencing an abusive man

And you went to talk to her but she doesn't listen to you,

Then you began to ask yourself

"What must I do? How do I tell my child that this man doesn't love you?

Because if he did, he wouldn't abuse you.

Anytime a man feels like he has to hit you,

It's all about trying to have control over you,

So he can always tell you what to do.

That's not love, its abuse!

When you accept a man abuse,

That's an unhealthy lifestyle for you and sometimes it can cause a break down

Within your body too.

Just know that the love of God can restore health back to you.

God is the man that created you

You were not created for a man abuse."

Even though the enemy has that child blind and can't see,

I'm learning that the power of prayer is the key,

To break the generational curse off our family.

He will give you strength to stand and pray,

And let the devil know that he still can't have his way.

Prayer will protect them

Because the truth is, the enemy is out to kill them.

# Mama Knows

Have you ever been through a storm where this man is abusing your daughter?

And you don't know what to do?

You find yourself upset with her because she keeps allowing him to.

Then she has the nerve to tell you, "Mind your own business."

But that seems too hard for you to do.

I'm talking about a child that could belong to me or you.

You find yourself praying to the Lord to break this strong hold a loose,

From the blind child who has accept a man's abuse.

And a mother knows because she has experienced that pain of abuse too.

A mother heart just wants the best for you

and you may think that she's only trying to live your life for you

But that's not true.

She just knows that living an abusive life isn't healthy for you

And that's how much love your mother has for you.

# Life Is a Journey

It is truly a blessing when God wake you up to see another day

Count it a blessing in spite of life's tests,

He will give you the strength you need to stand up and hold your head.

Learn not to be a person that complains about everything.

I'm learning how to be thankful for the sunshine and rain.

Pray that your circumstances are subject to change.

Life is a journey for you and me

Do you know that all of us have a personal journey to achieve?

Faith will help us to trust and believe.

Whatever our hand touch will succeed.

Have faith and just believe.

Living for Christ there is a price,

You will have to make some sacrifices.

You will be disliked and hated without a cause

That's one of the responsibilities of being a Christian.

By reaching out for the ones that are lost.

# No Weapon

He will give you the peace that pasts all understanding

In the midst of the storm, he will never leave nor forsake you,

In spite of the situation you may be going through.

Just know that whatever weapon comes against you, it shall not prosper

Because of the love that the father has for me and for you.

There's power in the word for you

To use when the enemy comes to use and abuse

Our father has already settles it in heaven

Pray that you won't stoop down to the devil level

# The Word Changes

The word comes in our life to purify and clean

The word with help us to accomplish our god given dreams

Life is filled with so many different things

But without him it is impossible to accomplish our god given dreams

Don't allow people to limit you

About what you can and cannot do

Dream big! Because he wants you to.

In spite of anyone's opinion of you

Dream big and see just what he will do.

# Recover It All

I will encourage you

that everything the enemy has stolen from you

Our God has the power to restore it all back to you

Learn how to keep the faith

And allow him to lead and guide you the right way

Even if you might be experiencing a little bit of darkness along the way

Just know that the light will shine from day to day

# Laughter Is Like Medicine

What will laughter do

If you take out the time and laugh too.

It will release the stress and pressure

That the spirit of Satan has attached to you

Know what it means when someone says, laughter is like a medicine for me and you

If you don't believe it go and get your bible and just read it.

Proverbs 15:13

# The Sun Will Shine

That is when you began to experience an over shower of blessings coming your way,

Every time you turn around, he blesses you to see a brighter day.

Open doors you will walk through

Is part of his plan and purpose for you

And people will see his favor all over you

It will help the doubter to believe in our savior too.

# Gifts

Your gifts will make room for you

to accomplish what Christ has created and ordained for
you to do

to help others in the world like me and you

these gifts only come from heaven above

because of his true love

only he can give

so we can live

love is the key

into eternity

# Power to Stand

Learn how to stand when you don't know what to do

Stand when you don't have a clue

Even when some people turn their backs on you

But you thought they would have wanted the very best for you

When the truth is they were secretly hating on you

You have the power within you

To stand for what's right and true

And the power to love your secret haters too.

# Don't Count Me Out

People may be trying to count you out

If you don't have a PhD

Or a Master Degree

And seem like you're not so smart in theology

When you or me accept Christ in our life

He will give you wisdom to explore and know more

So don't count me out or shut the door

What he gave you and what he gave me

Let us put it together and watch it succeed

I need you and you need me

Together we stand, divided we fall

He didn't give one person all

So here on earth his work will be done

That's why he gave his only begotten son

# Personal Storms

Storms that the Lord has truly graced me and has strengthen me to get through, the passing of some of my loved ones that I miss very much. If it had not been for his grace, I couldn't have run this race. We as the people of the Lord have to learn to how to keep the faith in all situations in life. I would have lost my mind but God who is rich and mercy has been protecting my mind, all this time. I know from personal experience, healing does take time, it is a process, so whatever you're going through just know that his love and power is within you. Experiencing a broken heart felt like my insides had been pulled apart. When my father passed, he passed on my birthday December 15, 2007, I was so devastated and heartbroken; it was breathtaking in this unexpected situation. I found myself being selfish in this situation, in my life because when you're a Daddy's Girl, it seems like this has messed up your whole world. Selfishness will blind you to the truth. I didn't realize that he was suffering with so much pain now the Lord knows best, I do believe that he's in everlasting rest. Before he left, I know within my heart he was heavenly bound. RIP Dad Milton Green Sr.

On February 8, 2011, my mother Lue Dessie Green passed on went home to be with the Lord breaking my heart once again, but I am thankful to know that she was born again. I am a firm believer that when you're saved and the Lord calls you home, you're going to see your loved ones again because the Lord does say to be absent from the body is to be present with the Lord.

Another storm for me and my youngest daughters, Mikessia Greeen and Kalandis Green, their grandmother passed away on December 10, 2013 and the amazing thing about this is that they had her home going service on December 15, 2013. Wow right? My birthday. That was the day that the Lord blessed me to see the age 47. I am 49 now. I know that I am blessed and highly favored by him. I know that I wouldn't be here if it wasn't for his mercy and grace, he has promised me long life, I can say I am truly thankful through it all. He has been good to me and my family because we are still standing by his grace. I begin to wonder what was so special about the month of December. Experiencing a whole lot of heartache and pain but by the grace so God, he didn't allow me to go insane. I'm learning how to be thankful for the storm and the rain. But then I had another experience, my brother Sammy passed December 23, 2013, 2 days before Christmas. I began to cry out from deep within my soul. I didn't understand why all of this was happening to me. Then the Lord spoke to me, he said, "Daughter, remember one of your desires was for your family and friends to be saved before they left this earth." I was like Yes! The he said to me, "I'm fulling one of your desires that I promised you." I do know that he has great plans for my life because if it had not been for his grace and mercy, I wouldn't have the ability to encourage others. See, through it all, he has been good to me. From personal experiences, he is a heart mender and when you fall, he's a head lifter and a life giver. My life has not been the same since. Now before all of this happened, our family had made plans to cook Christmas dinner together. My brother was going to prepare the turkey and the greens, because the boy can cook. Now I am the sister that always prepare the chicken dressing, potato salad, baking the pies and cooking the BBQ sometimes. My oldest daughter Jacqueline who prepare some BBQ meat too. But after this happened, it was like all the strength I had, had left out of me. I began to bend over with head down and say, "Lord help me please!" I was hurting so deep down inside, I knew that he heard my inner cry. I felt his peace all of me, from the top of head to soles of my feet. In this darkest hour, you see, he has been the shield and protection for me and my family. Because the month of December has been a testing time for our family. One Sunday I didn't make it to service, so my uncle Sylvester told me that my brother had sung a song for the whole church to hear. So I asked him to sing it for me, it really did amaze me to hear him sing this song. I never knew he could sing; I believe the Lord gave him that particular song to sing to minister to the whole congregation. The name of the song is "I Can See Clearly Now". The things that I have experienced caused me to grow in such an amazing way, that I know that I wouldn't be the person I am today. If it had not been for the experiences I had to endure. I had to experience some hardships in life that I found myself not wanting to do. I had to pray that the Lord will strengthen me through it because out of all of the burials, of my loved ones, he graced me to pick out their last wearing of clothes. Because of him I didn't lose my mind. That's why it's very important to have a mind of Christ in this world called life. The Lord blessed my oldest brother George to live to see the age 53, it did seem likely he left us so quickly. He passed away July 15, 2015; my heart broken again, but Jesus, who is my best friend, because of his grace and mercy, he mended my heart once again. Now the responsibility of the burial was not on me, God gave his oldest daughter, my niece Teresa, the strength to stand. He helped her to face reality. It wasn't easy for her to do but she realized who gave her the strength to.

# God Will Deliver

My son was incarcerated the year of 2014. Prayer will and prayer can change any situation in life. He had been in prison almost 2 years but by God's grace and mercy kept him protected and safe. He was released 3 days before my 49th birthday, December 12, 2015! He didn't supposed to get released until February 2016, my God is good and faithful to his word. All glory belongs to God. AMEN

# Healings

On January 3, 2016 I went to my beautician to get my hair done, she can do some hair. I think that's one of her gifts so after she finished my hair, she began to experience some muscle spasms. So, I told her to sit down and relax but she couldn't because the pain was going through her leg into her foot. So, I obey God and kneeled down and laid hands on her and prayed. God healed her instantly from muscle spasms! She walked through the house giving him all the raise and I was blessed to rejoice with her. Praise God! All glory belongs to him. AMEN

I have experienced the healing power of God on many different occasions. I have a daughter that the doctor said she have 2 cysts on her ovaries. I obeyed the Lord and laid hands on her stomach. I prayed for him to heal her and her did by removing both of them from her ovaries. The anointing of healing is so powerful. Praise God! All glory belongs to him. AMEN

I have another daughter that was threatening a stroke but the power of God healed her instantly. It didn't paralyze her at all and she's still standing by the grace of God. Praise God! AMEN

# Miracle's Healing

Born April 27, 2009, I have a niece and they call her Miracle. The doctors said that Miracle's mother was high-risk while carrying her, they didn't think Miracle was going to make it because they said she only have 1 kidney and there weren't any fluids but prayer turned that situation around. God blessed her with 2 kidneys and fluids begin to show up in her body so that's why we call

her Miracle because she's truly a miracle. Praise God!
AMEN

# ATA

I was born December 15, 1966, in Hayti, Mo. To the late Milton Green Sr. and Lue D. Green. I became a single mother at the age of 16. I didn't have a clue how to take care of my baby or what I should do. I was a young and immature little girl who was out there looking for love, but I later found out that it was only the lust of my flesh and because of the choice I made, I was hard-headed and didn't accept the wisdom my parents gave. This cost me to have a baby at a very young age. I have truly learned that what doesn't kill you in life only makes you stronger, and to be grateful to the Lord for not letting it destroy you through the process. It's truly a blessing to reach out to others. I am now a mother of 6; 5 daughters: Jacqueline, Kimberly, Stephanie Mikessia and Kalandis, and one son, Jack. I have three more children from another mother: Kimberly V., Sharika and Jack Jr., and I love them the same as if they were mine. I also have one god-son, Darius. One of my daughters was diagnosed with ADHD, God healed her and now she is grown and has been blessed with a beautiful daughter of her own. Now, because of who God is, I am blessed to tell the world my story about how I made it over and did not lose my mind through the process. I'm a grandmother of nine, Jamien, Ja'Nyia, Ja'Markus, Jaylen, Bry'Onna, Ja'Kylah, Ja'Marko, Ja'Mya and Ja'Nasia. They have brought so much joy in my life and I am so thankful for knowing who my savior is. I am expecting a new healthy grandbaby next year, she will make number ten! I am a CNA, an overcomer of rape and abuse, all glory belongs to God. Today I can say, I'm not a victim, I'm a victor. Amen.

# BLURB

Pain is real. I know I'm sharing the things that the Lord has brought me through. I know in my heart that there are many people out in the world today who are hurting like I was. Death is something that we all will experience, and maybe there are other things in your life that you are going through. It took God in my life to get me through, but first you have to get to know him and remember that you aren't alone. He is able! I am here to encourage you from biblical example and my own personal experiences, trusting in Him is a process of growth. He is a presence help in the time of our needs. I am a living witness if you choose to walk by faith, he will strengthen you to run your race. I am still standing because of his mercy and grace.

Made in the USA
Columbia, SC
10 February 2025